IRAN

Madeline Donaldson

Lerner Publications Company • Minneapolis

Lerner Publications Company
A division of Lerner Publishing Group, Inc.
241 First Avenue North
Minneapolis, MN 55401 U.S.A.

Website address: www.lernerbooks.com

Library of Congress Cataloging-in-Publication Data

Donaldson, Madeline.
    Iran / by Madeline Donaldson.
      p.   cm. — (Country explorers)
    Includes index.
    ISBN 978–1–58013–606–8 (lib. bdg. : alk. paper)
    1. Iran—Juvenile literature. I. Title.
DS254.75.D66 2010
955—dc22   2009019479

Manufactured in the United States of America
1 – VI – 12/15/09

Table of Contents

Welcome!

At last! We've reached Iran. This large country is in southwestern Asia. Iran shares borders with seven countries and three bodies of water. Iraq and Turkey lie west of Iran. Pakistan and Afghanistan are Iran's eastern neighbors. The Caspian Sea lies to the north. To the south are the Persian Gulf and the Gulf of Oman.

The Caspian Sea lies north of Iran.

4

AZERBAIJAN

ARMENIA
• Tabriz

CASPIAN
SEA

TURKMENISTAN

N

MILES
0   200
0   200
KILOMETERS

SAFID RIVER

ELBURZ MTNS.

CASPIAN LOWLANDS

• Mashhad

★ **Tehran**

MOUNT
DAMAVAND

AFGHANISTAN

ZAGROS

DASHT-E-KAVIR

I R A N

★ country's capital

lowlands

deserts

plains

mountains

ancient site

ZAYANDEH RIVER

PLATEAU

OF

IRAN

• Esfahan

KARUN RIVER

IRAQ

KHUZESTAN
PLAIN

MOUNTAINS

Persepolis

• Shiraz

DASHT-E-LUT

PAKISTAN

PERSIAN
GULF

GULF OF OMAN

Many Landforms

Iran has many different landscapes. Mountains rise in the north and west. A high plateau, or flat area, sits in the center. Bordering the plateau are huge deserts. Iran also has some lowlands along the Caspian Sea, the Persian Gulf, and the Gulf of Oman.

Mountains rise behind these wheat fields in Iran.

6

Map Whiz Quiz

Take a look at the map on page 5. A map is a drawing or chart of a place. Trace the outline of Iran on a sheet of paper. Can you find the Caspian Sea? Mark this part of your map with an *N* for north. How about Iraq? Mark this part with a *W* for west. Look for the Persian Gulf. Mark it with an *S* for south. Finally, find Afghanistan. Mark it with an *E* for east. With a green crayon, color in Iran. Color the Caspian Sea, the Persian Gulf, and the Gulf of Oman blue.

Families swim in the Caspian Sea. The Caspian Sea is the world's largest inland water body. Inland water bodies don't flow into the ocean.

7

The Plateau of Iran

Central Iran is huge. The Plateau of Iran stands out in this part of the country. The area is hot in summer. Temperatures rise as high as 120°F (50°C). Winters are mild. But nights are cool.

A woman walks on a desert in Iran.

Deserts hug the northeast and southeast edges of the plateau. The deserts are called Dasht-e-Kavir and Dasht-e-Lut. The Dasht-e-Kavir is salty. The Dasht-e-Lut is sandy. Strong sandstorms keep people, animals, and plants from living there.

Date palms grow in this oasis in the Dasht-e-Kavir.

9

High Up

Over time, movement took place under the ground of Iran. The movement made the edges of the plateau fold over one another. The folds kept pushing upward. Slowly, two mountain ranges formed. The Zagros Mountains spread along the western side of Iran.

Clouds surround the high peaks of the Zagros Mountains.

Another range—the Elburz Mountains—curves around the Caspian Sea. The mountains get a lot of snow in winter. Summers are warm but not too hot.

Tehran

Tehran is the capital of Iran. The city spreads out south of the Elburz Mountains. The country's highest point is Mount Damavand. It can be seen from almost anywhere in the city.

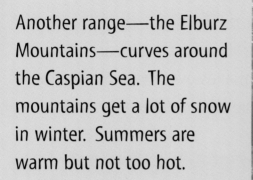

These buildings in Tehran lie at the foot of the Elburz Mountains.

11

Shaking Earth

Far below the plateau's moving folds, the earth is burning hot. It churns and bubbles. It's not solid. The earth shifts. That shifting causes shakes and buckles. The results are earthquakes. Iran has many earthquakes every year. Not all of them cause damage. But some have destroyed entire villages.

Two children stand in rubble from an earthquake. The earthquake destroyed many houses.

The Red Crescent

The Red Crescent

After an earthquake, members of Iran's Red Crescent spring into action. They send food, water, medicine, and other emergency help. They bring in sniffer dogs. The dogs help find people who are trapped. The Red Crescent sets up camps and hospitals for survivors.

Red Crescent workers give medicine to people in need.

These students learn how to make houses strong enough to last through earthquakes.

13

Along the Seas

Narrow strips of land border the Caspian Sea, the Persian Gulf, and the Gulf of Oman. The land in these areas is low, close to the level of the sea. Some of it can be farmed. In the Caspian Lowlands, farmers raise rice, tea, wheat, and barley. The weather there is mild year-round. This area also gets the most rain.

This rice field is in the Caspian Lowlands. Rice needs a lot of water to grow.

14

The Khuzestan Plain is at the
northern end of the Persian Gulf.
Most of Iran's oil fields lie there.
Summers on the plain are hot
and humid. But winters are
mild and warm.

Oil

Oil was first found in Iran in the
early 1900s. Since then, the
country has become the world's
fourth-largest producer of oil.
Ships filled with oil chug down
the Persian Gulf. Then they
pass through the Gulf of Oman.
Finally, they reach the Arabian
Sea and the open ocean.

Oil tankers and
other large ships are
a common sight in
Iran's waters.

Long-Ago Iran

People have been living in Iran for many years. It was the home of the great Persian Empire. This empire was at its largest more than 2,500 years ago! It went as far east as Pakistan. It reached as far west as North Africa and Greece.

Persepolis

The capital of the Persian Empire was Persepolis. The ruins of the city sit in southwestern Iran. The city had grand palaces and meeting halls. Its great wealth showed the world the empire's power.

Visitors to Iran can see some of the buildings of Persepolis.

About 2,300 years ago, the first outsiders took over the area. Outsiders ruled for hundreds of years. A break in foreign rule took place from about 1500 to 1800. After that, Iran stayed under foreign rule until the 1920s.

Persian Cats

Members of the Persian royal family kept cats as pets. The cats had long hair and flat faces. Persian cats are among the world's most popular cats.

This stone carving shows two soldiers at Persepolis.

Iranians

The people of Iran belong to different ethnic groups. About half of the population is Persian. They come from the people who lived in Iran thousands of years ago. This group uses Persian as its main language. It is also called Farsi.

Many children speak Persian, or Farsi, at school.

Some of Iran's other ethnic groups are also found in neighboring countries. The Azeris, for example, share a history with people in Azerbaijan. The Kurds have ties to people in Turkey and Iraq. The Baluchis are kin to a people in Pakistan. Iran is also home to a small number of Arabs. All these groups speak their own languages. They also speak Persian.

The Lur

Iran's Lur people are herders. They travel within the mountain valleys. There, they find water and grazing land for their goats and sheep.

A family of herders cares for their sheep.

Inside Tehran University, Iranian women pray.

Following Islam

Millions of people follow the religion of Islam. They are called Muslims. Most Iranians are Muslims. Iranian Muslims pray five times daily to Allah (God). And they celebrate Muslim holidays throughout the year.

Beautiful tiles adorn the front of the Nasir al-Molk Mosque.

Historic Places

Iran has many historic mosques. A mosque is an Islamic place of worship. The city of Shiraz holds the Nasir al-Molk Mosque. Its beautiful tiles and brilliant stained glass draw many visitors. The Shaykh Lutfallah Mosque sits in Esfahan. This city is in central Iran. The main entrance to the mosque is decorated with rich, blue tiles. Every year, millions of Muslims visit Mashhad, a city in northeastern Iran. They go to the grave of Imam Reza. He was a Muslim leader who died in that city.

The Best Eids

Muslims throughout Iran honor the holy month of Ramadan. They fast during this time. They do not eat or drink between sunrise and sunset. When the month ends, Muslims hold a special festival called Eid al-Fitr. Children get gifts. Families get together for a special meal.

An Iranian girl smiles during Eid al-Fitr.

22

Men and boys gather at mosques to pray during Eid-e-Ghorban. This festival honors the prophet Abraham. He was willing to give up his son to obey Allah. Other Muslim festivals honor the prophet Muhammad, who founded Islam.

A Lunar Calendar

Iran uses a lunar calendar for Islamic holidays. A lunar calendar is based on the movement of the moon. In a lunar calendar, holiday dates are ten to twelve days earlier than the year before. For example, Eid al-Fitr fell on September 21 in 2009. It will take place around September 11 in 2010.

Men gather in Tehran for the Eid-e-Ghorban prayers.

More Ways to Celebrate

Iranians also celebrate non-Islamic holidays. In late March, they are joyful on Noruz. This time marks the coming of spring and the Iranian New Year. Iranian kids love Noruz. They get gifts, usually money or candy. They don't have to be in school. Families and friends get together to share food. And everyone wears new clothes. At the end of Noruz, families go to a park for a picnic.

Noruz means "new day." Each of the foods served at Noruz has a special meaning.

24

Iranians also honor dates linked to Ruholla Khomeini. This Muslim leader founded modern Iran in 1979. Iranians celebrate the founding on April 1. They also honor the day of Khomeini's death on June 4, 1989.

Iranians have holidays that honor Ruholla Khomeini.

A group of Muslim men talk in Parsi.

Parsi or Farsi?

Iran's official language, Persian, is written using Arabic lettering. Arabic is the language of Islam. People who speak Persian call their language Parsi. But Arabic has no sound for *P*. So in Arabic, the name sounds like *Farsi*. Iranians added letters to Arabic writing to stand for the sounds of *P*, *G*, and *CH*.

Words in English and Persian

English	Persian	Pronunciation
hello	salaam	sah-LAHM
good-bye	khoda hafez	hoh-dah-FEHZ
please	lotfan	loht-FAHN
thank you	motshakeram	moht-shy-keh-RAHM

Parsi is part of the Indo-European family of languages. French, English, and Italian are part of this family too.

27

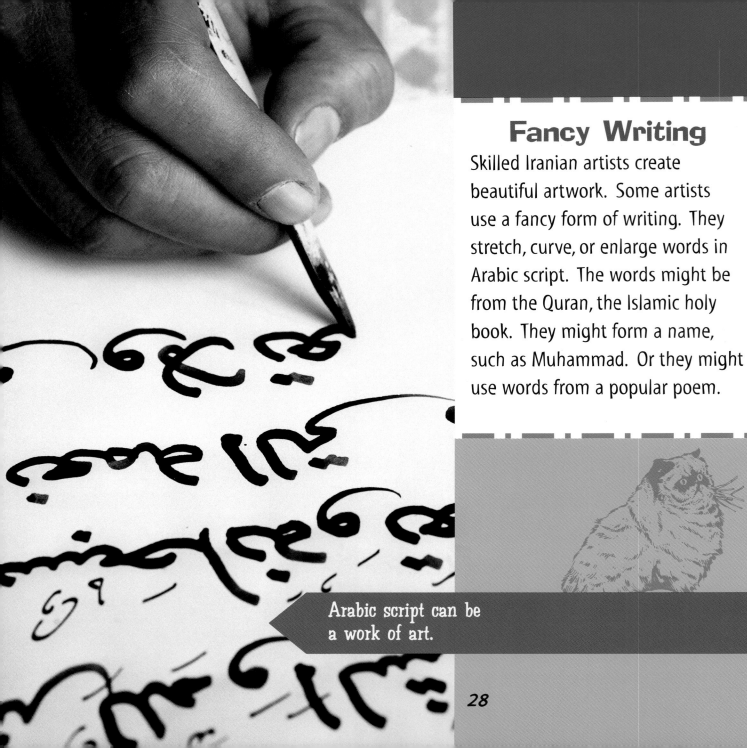

Fancy Writing

Skilled Iranian artists create beautiful artwork. Some artists use a fancy form of writing. They stretch, curve, or enlarge words in Arabic script. The words might be from the Quran, the Islamic holy book. They might form a name, such as Muhammad. Or they might use words from a popular poem.

Arabic script can be a work of art.

28

Popular Poets

Iranians honor poets old and new. Poet and math whiz Omar Khayyam lived in the 1100s. His famous *Rubaiyat* is a collection of many four-line poems. The work is admired within and beyond Iran. Another poet, Saadi, lived in the 1200s. He wrote *Golestan* (*The Rose Garden*). The tales celebrate honesty, respect, and quick thinking. Hafez lived in the 1300s. He is known for his deeply personal poems.

This Quran was created more than eight hundred years ago.

All in the Family

The father is the head of the family in Iran. He helps find his children marriage partners and jobs. Iranian children are close to their mothers. A mother makes sure her children feel valued and loved. Grandparents, aunts, uncles, and cousins are also close. Family businesses may bring together the youngest to the oldest members. The whole family works hard to take care of one another.

A large extended family shares a meal.

Young and Old

Iranians honor the oldest people in their family. On holidays, elders are greeted first. They get the best seats at the table. And they are offered the tastiest food. Iran also has a high population of young people. Nearly one of every three Iranians is fifteen or younger.

A family in Iran enjoys a picnic in a park.

School

Iranian children start school at about the age of seven. They spend five years in elementary school. Girls and boys go to separate schools. Iran doesn't have enough school buildings. Schools often run in two shifts—morning and afternoon. The shifts allow all kids to go to school.

It is the first day of school for these girls in Tehran.

At the end of elementary school, students take a test. Those who pass go on to three years of middle school. There, teachers help kids think about their skills and interests. This helps them plan for high school or college or for getting a job.

A class of Iranian boys watches a classmate write on the board.

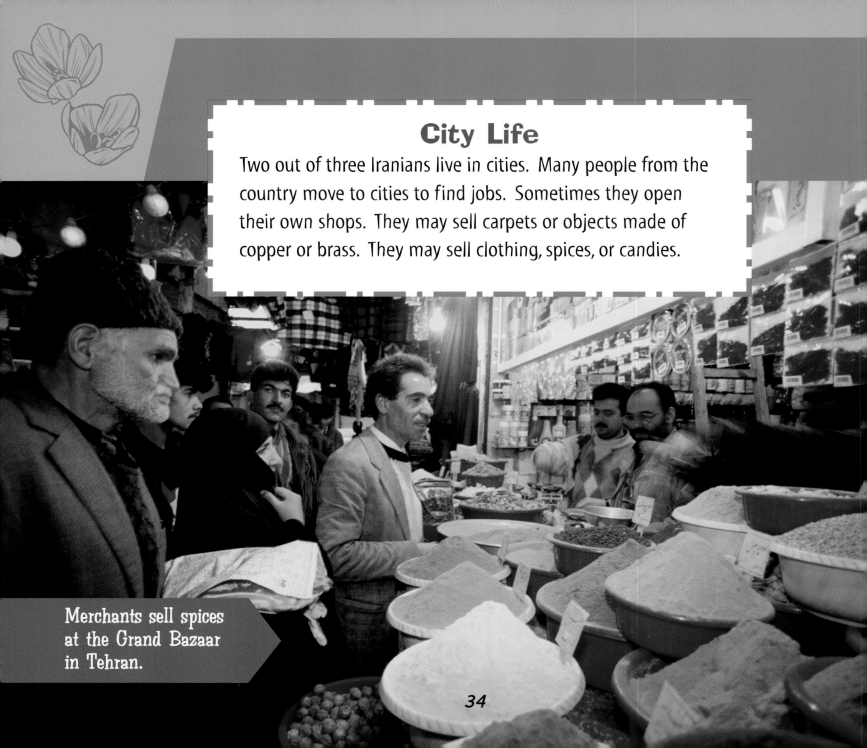

City Life

Two out of three Iranians live in cities. Many people from the country move to cities to find jobs. Sometimes they open their own shops. They may sell carpets or objects made of copper or brass. They may sell clothing, spices, or candies.

Merchants sell spices at the Grand Bazaar in Tehran.

Iran's biggest city is Tehran. Long, wide streets and tall modern buildings are everywhere. The capital also has museums, markets, and a huge outdoor sports stadium. Other big cities include Tabriz, Mashhad, Esfahan, and Shiraz.

Dear Aunt Mary,

Dad and I just got back from Azadi Stadium in Tehran. We went to see a soccer match between two Iranian teams, Persepolis and Esteghlal. The stadium can seat up to 100,000 people! The noise was amazing! See you soon!

Josh

Aunt Ma

Your To

Anywhere

Country Life

About one out of three Iranians lives in the country. Many farm the land or raise livestock. Children often help with this work. They also help with other chores, such as taking care of younger children. Villagers, especially girls and women, may make goods to sell. They may sew clothes or make carpets. Rural areas have fewer schools. As a result, a lot of rural kids don't go past elementary school.

A woman smooths the walls of her house with mud. Some houses in Iran are made of mud.

Persian Carpets

Woolen carpets from Iran are world famous. The best ones are made by hand. Each woolen thread is woven through a web and knotted. The carpets can take months to finish.

Housing in the country is simple. One-level homes with flat roofs might be made of mud bricks. The homes stay cool in the hot summers. They often have only a couple of windows. Owners brighten up the homes. Sometimes they paint the doors bright colors. They hang colorful carpets on the walls.

This man uses a loom to weave a carpet.

Let's Eat!

Iranians love to eat together. Lunch is the main meal. Sometimes lunch leftovers make up the evening meal. Cooks take pride in finding the freshest foods. They take time to present their finished dishes in a pleasing way.

A woman carefully prepares food in her kitchen.

38

Iranians serve stews of lamb or chicken and vegetables over rice. They also enjoy fresh fish from the Caspian Sea. Salads and yogurt are popular. Mint, basil, saffron, and cloves are popular herbs and spices. They give the dishes a delicious flavor. Naan, a flat bread, is always on hand. Fresh fruit and nuts are favorite desserts. But Iranian kids are crazy about ice cream!

Saffron

Iran supplies nearly all the world's saffron. This spice is bright yellow. It is made from the spiky stamens in the center of the crocus flower. Each flower makes only three stamens. So it takes thousands of flowers to create just a little bit of saffron.

Ice cream is a favorite treat among Iranian children.

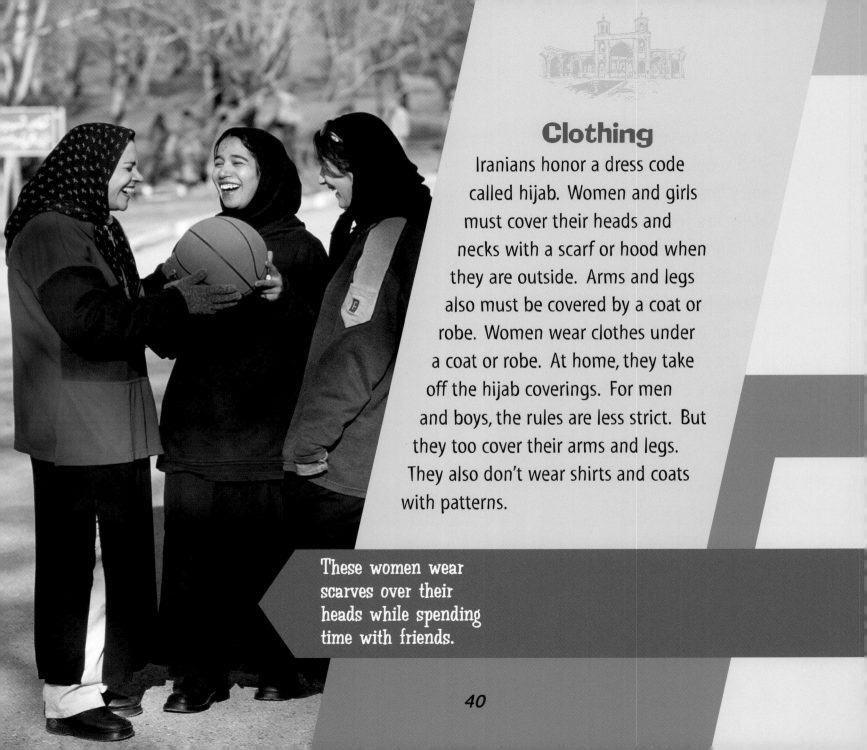

Clothing

Iranians honor a dress code called hijab. Women and girls must cover their heads and necks with a scarf or hood when they are outside. Arms and legs also must be covered by a coat or robe. Women wear clothes under a coat or robe. At home, they take off the hijab coverings. For men and boys, the rules are less strict. But they too cover their arms and legs. They also don't wear shirts and coats with patterns.

These women wear scarves over their heads while spending time with friends.

Having a dress code doesn't stop Iranians from going out. They go shopping and gather at parks. Movie theaters draw crowds. Grown-ups go to work. They might work at shops, restaurants, offices, or building sites.

Men watch a chess game in a park in Iran.

Sports and Games

Soccer rules the sports scene in Iran. The national team competes well against teams from other countries. Iran also has a professional soccer league. Persepolis and Esteghlal are the biggest rivals.

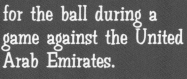

Esteghlal player Pejman Montazeri (*left*) runs for the ball during a game against the United Arab Emirates.

Wrestling and weight lifting have long been popular. Iran has won several Olympic medals in both sports. Some people think polo (a field game played on horses) and the board game chess came from Iran.

Olympic Medals

Iranian athlete Hadi Saei won gold medals at the 2004 and 2008 Summer Olympics. He won in the martial arts sport of tae kwon do. He also won a bronze medal at the 2000 Sydney Olympics. These medals put him at the top of Iran's Olympic winners' list.

Hadi Saei kisses his gold medal at the 2008 Olympics.

THE FLAG OF IRAN

Iran's flag has a green, a white, and a red stripe. Green is a color tied to Islam. The white stripe stands for peace. Red stands for courage. The center symbol is made up of four half-moon shapes, called crescents, and a sword. The crescents stand for Allah. The sword stands for strength. Above and below the crescents are words in Arabic. They repeat the prayer *Allahu Akbar*. These words mean "God is great."

FAST FACTS

FULL COUNTRY NAME: Islamic Republic of Iran

AREA: 636,296 square miles (1,648,007 square kilometers), or a bit smaller than the state of Alaska

MAIN LANDFORMS: the mountains Elburz and Zagros, the Caspian seacoast, the Plateau of Iran, the deserts Dasht-e-Kavir and Dasht-e-Lut, and the Khuzestan Plain

MAJOR RIVERS: Karun, Safid, and Zayandeh

ANIMALS AND THEIR HABITATS: Persian gazelle and the Iranian bee-eater (plateau); ibex and larks (desert); leopards, bearded vulture, and Mesopotamian deer (mountains); gray-necked bunting and wild boar (forests and grasslands); fish, including sturgeon, whitefish, and herring (Caspian Sea)

CAPITAL CITY: Tehran

OFFICIAL LANGUAGE: Farsi (Persian)

POPULATION: 71.2 million

GLOSSARY

desert: a dry region that can be sandy or salty

ethnic group: a large community of people that shares the same language, religion, and customs

goods: things to sell

Islam: a religion that began in Saudi Arabia. Followers of Islam pray to Allah.

map: a drawing or chart of all or part of Earth or the sky

mosque: an Islamic place of worship

mountain: a part of Earth's surface that rises high into the sky

Muslim: a person who follows Islam

oasis: a moist, green spot in a desert

plateau: a high, flat area of land

Quran: the Islamic holy book

stamen: a long, skinny spike that helps a flower to make more flowers

valley: an area of lowland that gets its water from a large river

TO LEARN MORE

BOOKS

Douglass, Susan L. *Ramadan*. Minneapolis: Millbrook Press, 2004. Learn about the month of Ramadan, during which Muslims honor Allah.

Downing, David. *Iran*. New York: Marshall Cavendish, 2008. Learn about the modern challenges Iran faces.

Haskins, Jim, and Kathleen Benson. *Count Your Way through Iran*. Minneapolis: Millbrook Press, 2007. Get to know Iran and its language through the numbers one through ten.

Mobin-Uddin, Asma. *The Best Eid Ever*. Honesdale, PA: Boyds Mills Press, 2007. This book tells the story of a girl's celebration of Eid al-Adha with her grandmother.

Price, Massoume. *Ancient Iran*. Vancouver, BC: Anahita Productions, 2008. Enjoy the splendor of long-ago Iran.

Schemenauer, Elma. *Welcome to Iran*. Mankato, MN: Child's World, 2008. Learn more about the people and places of Iran in this book.

WEBSITES

Enchanted Learning: World Geography
http://www.enchantedlearning.com/geography
This site has pages about Iran and an outline map of the country.

World Exploration
https://www.cia.gov/kids-page/games/world-exploration/index.html
Take a fun geography quiz from the Central Intelligence Agency.

INDEX